SPACE
CRUSADERS

Sally Ride

Trailblazing Astronaut

Rebecca Felix

**Checkerboard
Library**

An Imprint of Abdo Publishing
abdobooks.com

ABDOBOOKS.COM

Published by Abdo Publishing, a division of ABDO, PO Box 398166, Minneapolis, Minnesota 55439.
Copyright © 2019 by Abdo Consulting Group, Inc. International copyrights reserved in all countries.
No part of this book may be reproduced in any form without written permission from the publisher.
Checkerboard Library™ is a trademark and logo of Abdo Publishing.

Printed in the United States of America, North Mankato, Minnesota
102018
012019

THIS BOOK CONTAINS
RECYCLED MATERIALS

Design: Kelly Doudna, Mighty Media, Inc.
Production: Mighty Media, Inc.
Editor: Jessie Alkire
Front Cover Photographs: NASA (both)
Back Cover Photographs: NASA (Aldrin, ISS, space shuttle, Apollo rocket), Shutterstock (planets)
Interior Photographs: AP Images, pp. 19, 23, 29 (bottom); NASA, pp. 5, 11, 13, 15, 17 (left, center, right), 21, 27, 28 (top),
29 (top left); NASA/Glenn Research Center, p. 9; Sally Ride Science/NASA, p. 29 (top right); Shutterstock, p. 25;
Yearbook Library, pp. 7, 28 (bottom)

Library of Congress Control Number: 2018948537

Publisher's Cataloging-in-Publication Data
Names: Felix, Rebecca, author.
Title: Sally Ride: trailblazing astronaut / by Rebecca Felix.
Other title: Trailblazing astronaut
Description: Minneapolis, Minnesota : Abdo Publishing, 2019 | Series: Space
    crusaders | Includes online resources and index.
Identifiers: ISBN 9781532117046 (lib. bdg.) | ISBN 9781532159886 (ebook)
Subjects: LCSH: Ride, Sally--Juvenile literature. | Astronauts--United States--
    Biography--Juvenile literature. | Women astronauts--Biography--Juvenile
    literature. | Women in engineering--United States--Biography--Juvenile
    literature.
Classification: DDC 629.450 [B]--dc23

Contents

Standout Space Explorer · · · · · · · · · · 4

School and Sports · · · · · · · · · · 6

Joining NASA · · · · · · · · · · 10

In the Spotlight · · · · · · · · · · 12

First Flight · · · · · · · · · · 14

More Missions · · · · · · · · · · 16

New Roles · · · · · · · · · · 18

Sally Ride Science · · · · · · · · · · 20

Honors and Hardship · · · · · · · · · · 22

Identity and Empowerment · · · · · · · · · · 24

Lasting Impact · · · · · · · · · · 26

Timeline · · · · · · · · · · 28

Glossary · · · · · · · · · · 30

Online Resources · · · · · · · · · · 31

Index · · · · · · · · · · 32

Standout Space Explorer

Sally Ride was a trailblazing astronaut. She was the first US woman to travel into space! This made Ride famous. But being a pioneering astronaut was just one of Ride's many successes. She was also a star student, a skilled **physicist**, and a talented athlete.

Ride studied physics in college and earned several degrees. When she applied to become an astronaut, **NASA** chose her out of thousands of applicants. The organization asked Ride to serve on special committees throughout her life.

Ride also served in several other science-based organizations. She started her own science education program for kids and wrote children's books about space. Ride's intelligence and leadership made her a standout in everything she did.

Although Ride stood out, she was a shy, quiet person. She was private about her personal life. It wasn't until after her death that the public learned Ride was gay. Ride has since become an important figure to the gay community. Her life's accomplishments blazed the trail for other female and gay space explorers.

2 School and Sports

Sally Kristen Ride was born on May 26, 1951, in Encino, California. She grew up in nearby Los Angeles. Sally's parents were Dale and Carol. Dale was a political science professor. Carol was a counselor.

When Sally was in fourth grade, her family spent a year traveling in Europe. When they returned, Sally entered sixth grade, skipping fifth grade. This was because Sally was ahead of her peers in reading and math. She also did very well in science.

Sally was talented in athletics too. She liked to run and play sports. Sally was a skilled tennis player. When she was 13, she met 12-year-old Tam O'Shaughnessy at tennis camp. The two developed a friendship that would last throughout their lives.

In 1964, Sally entered Westlake High School for Girls. She graduated in 1968 and **enrolled** in Swarthmore College in Pennsylvania. Sally attended the school for three **semesters** and then moved home. She missed California.

Ride then played tennis professionally for a short time. She earned a national ranking as a junior player. In 1970, Ride decided to go back to school. She enrolled in Stanford University

Ride credits her parents with encouraging her interest in science.

to study **physics** and English. But Ride didn't give up tennis. She played on the school's tennis team. She was Stanford's number one women's singles player in 1971.

Soon Ride began to focus more on studying than tennis in college. In 1973, she earned **bachelor's degrees** in both physics and English. At the time, not many women studied science or math. It was more common and accepted for men to be interested in math or science. Women were often discouraged from following careers in these fields. Ride was the only woman in her first college physics class.

After graduation, Ride continued studying physics at Stanford. In 1975, she earned a **master's degree** in the subject. Ride remained at Stanford and studied for a **PhD** in physics.

In 1977, Ride was reading a Stanford University newspaper when an advertisement caught her eye. **NASA** was looking for female astronauts! Until then, all astronauts had been male. Women weren't allowed to become astronauts until the 1970s.

As soon as Ride saw the NASA ad, she knew she wanted to become an astronaut. She tore the ad from the newspaper and applied that same day. That application would change her life and the course of history.

Ride was interested in space during school. But she didn't think she could become an astronaut because of her gender.

Joining NASA

About 8,000 men and women applied to be **NASA** astronauts. In January 1978, only 35 people were chosen for the program. Only six were women. Ride was one of them! Ride completed her **PhD** in **physics** from Stanford later that year. She soon began astronaut training.

Ride's training began on the ground. She helped build a robotic arm for space shuttles. Ride was noticed for her hard work and easygoing personality. These traits earned her a very important role. Ride was named capsule communicator (CAPCOM) on a ground-support crew for a shuttle flight in 1981 and another in 1982.

As CAPCOM, Ride was the only person on the ground at NASA to speak to the astronauts during missions. Ride did well in this role. NASA leaders took note of how calm Ride was under pressure.

In 1982, Russian astronaut Svetlana Savitskaya became the second woman in history to travel into space. Russia remained

STELLAR!

Russian astronaut Valentina Tereshkova was the first woman to travel into space. She orbited Earth 48 times in a spacecraft in 1963.

Ride (*left*) was NASA's first female capsule communicator (CAPCOM).

the only country to send a female into space. But Ride and
NASA would soon change this. NASA chose Ride as a crew
member for its 1983 STS-7 space mission.

4 In the Spotlight

As Ride prepared for her mission, changes were taking place in her personal life. In 1982, she married fellow astronaut Steven Hawley. At the time, Ride's upcoming spaceflight made her the focus of much **media** attention. But Ride and Hawley kept news of their marriage private. The media did not find out the two were married until one month after the ceremony.

The public was very interested in Ride's personal life. Ride was one of five STS-7 crew members, and the only woman. Her **gender** was a main point of interest for the press. But some reporters judged Ride. Many male reporters asked her **sexist** questions. These reporters suggested Ride was emotionally weaker than male astronauts. They asked her if she cried when facing problems in spaceflight training. Some reporters even asked if Ride would wear makeup in space.

Ride felt these reporters' questions were silly and unfair. She asked why her male crew members weren't asked the same things. Ride was disappointed that her gender overshadowed the science of the mission for some people. She said it was time the nation realized women could do any job they wanted.

Ride was joined by four men on the STS-7 mission. This was the first NASA spaceflight with five crew members. Previous missions had up to four crew members.

5 First Flight

Ride's upcoming spaceflight remained major national news. On June 18, 1983, a crowd of reporters gathered at Kennedy Space Center in Florida to watch Ride's historic launch. Ride's mother, father, sister, and friend O'Shaughnessy attended the launch too.

The launch was also televised. US journalist and **feminist** Gloria Steinem noted that millions of girls would be watching the launch on TV. And Ride would show them that they could be astronauts, explorers, and scientists.

When the crew was in place, the shuttle *Challenger* launched. Within 8.5 minutes, the shuttle was traveling at 17,500 miles per hour (28,164 kmh)! As *Challenger* left Earth's atmosphere, Ride became the first US woman in space. She was only the third woman in history to achieve spaceflight.

Ride acted as mission specialist for the STS-7 mission. In this role, she used a robotic arm to release **satellites** into space. She also helped complete several experiments onboard.

The STS-7 crew was in space for six days. *Challenger* returned to Earth on June 24.

STELLAR!
Ride enjoyed weightlessness in space. She described it as "just fun."

14

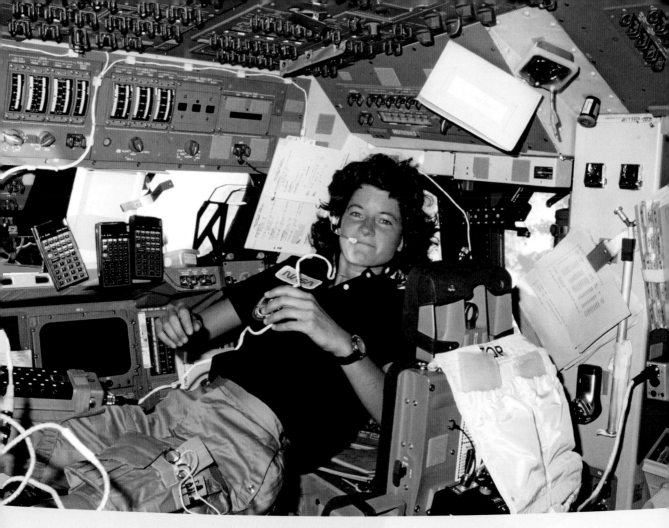

Ride described the *Challenger* launch as "exhilarating, terrifying, and overwhelming all at the same time."

Reporters couldn't wait to interview Ride. She told them of spaceflight, "I'm sure it was the most fun that I'll ever have in my life."

6 More Missions

Though Ride's historic spaceflight had ended, attention from the **media** continued. Ride was a role model to girls and women. She gave speeches at schools and organizations. She was also the subject of many media articles.

Ride also continued her career at **NASA**. On October 5, 1984, she went into space for a second time. This made Ride the first US woman in history to travel into space twice! Ride again acted as mission specialist.

This time, Ride was not the only female astronaut onboard the *Challenger*. Kathryn Sullivan was a fellow crew member on the mission, called STS-41G. The STS-41G crew was in space for eight days. In that time, they deployed another **satellite**, made scientific observations of Earth, and performed **space walks**.

Ride was scheduled to go into space for a third time. But on January 28, 1986, tragedy struck at NASA. That day, a different crew of astronauts boarded *Challenger*. The space shuttle exploded after liftoff. All seven crew members died. NASA put its space shuttle program on hold to work on safety issues. Ride's future spaceflight was canceled.

FEMALE ASTRONAUT FIRSTS

KATHRYN SULLIVAN (1951–)

+ First female astronaut to walk in space
+ Traveled into space three times
+ Became administrator of the National Oceanic and Atmospheric Administration

EILEEN COLLINS (1956–)

+ First female space shuttle pilot
+ First female space shuttle commander
+ First astronaut to fly the space shuttle through a complete 360-degree flip to capture photos from a new angle

PEGGY WHITSON (1960–)

+ First woman to command the International Space Station
+ Spent 666 hours in space, more time than any other female astronaut
+ First female Chief of the Astronaut Office at NASA, overseeing all astronaut activities

7 New Roles

With her role as astronaut on hold, Ride was offered a new position at **NASA**. She became part of a special committee formed to investigate the *Challenger* explosion. During the investigation, Ride discovered something alarming. Popular opinion was that *Challenger* had exploded because certain parts of the shuttle malfunctioned in cold weather. Ride read a report that suggested NASA knew this was possible before the explosion occurred.

Ride shared the report with another member of the committee. The public found out about the report too. Many people respected Ride for sharing the report. She helped reveal the truth even though it meant her coworkers at NASA could be in serious trouble.

NASA leaders also appreciated Ride's work on the investigation. When the committee ended, NASA made Ride the Special Assistant to the Administration at NASA Headquarters. In this role, Ride spent one year helping develop plans for NASA. Her plan was called the Ride Report. One idea in the plan was to

RUMMEL

EPH SUTTER

ARTHUR

SALLY RIDE

AL KEEL

ROGERS

Ride was the only woman on the committee that investigated the *Challenger* explosion. She was known for asking tough questions.

launch **satellites** that would monitor and record climate change effects on Earth.

In 1987, Ride left **NASA**. That same year, she and Hawley divorced. Ride's time as an astronaut was over. But her influence on science and space exploration was not.

Sally Ride Science

After leaving **NASA**, Ride took a job as director of the California Space Institute at the University of California in San Diego. In 1989, she also became a **physics** professor at the school.

Ride remained an important figure in space exploration. When Bill Clinton became the US president in the 1990s, he asked Ride to serve as the head of NASA. Ride turned the job down. She did not want to be in the public eye again.

In 1999, Ride served as the president of Space.com. This website provides information and photos related to the **cosmos** and space travel. Ride held the position for one year. In 2001, Ride, O'Shaughnessy, and three other friends started their own company called Sally Ride Science. Ride was president and CEO.

The goal of Sally Ride Science was to create educational programs and products for kids interested in math and science. Ride especially wanted to inspire young girls. Girls were still discouraged from choosing careers in math and science. Ride hoped to change this.

Since 2001, Sally Ride Science has organized more than 100 Sally Ride Science Festivals. These events support girls who want to study science and math.

Ride also wrote science books for children. She authored six books on different space and space exploration topics. O'Shaughnessy coauthored several of them.

9 Honors and Hardship

Ride stayed busy with her company and her writing. But when **NASA** asked for her help following a 2003 tragedy, she made time to do so. The space shuttle *Columbia* had launched into space on January 16. When *Columbia* reentered Earth's atmosphere on February 1, the shuttle disintegrated. All seven crew members died. NASA asked Ride to investigate the cause of the accident. The investigation determined the cause was a hole in the shuttle's **thermal** protection system.

NASA was not the only organization to recognize Ride's skills and knowledge. In 2003, Ride was the first woman to be admitted into the Astronaut Hall of Fame. In 2007, she was admitted into the National **Aviation** Hall of Fame.

When Barack Obama became the US president in 2008, he showed interest in making Ride head of NASA. But as Ride had told President Clinton in the 1990s, she did not want this public role. Ride remained a private person, sharing little personal information with the public.

Ride accepted the National Aviation Hall of Fame medal from Robert Crippen, a fellow astronaut. He was the commander on Ride's first NASA mission.

Identity and Empowerment

In 2010, Ride learned she had **cancer**. She died on July 23, 2012. The public was shocked. Only a few friends and family members had known Ride was sick.

People were surprised to learn something else about Ride after she died. In Ride's **obituary**, O'Shaughnessy was referred to as Ride's partner. Ride and O'Shaughnessy had been a couple for almost 30 years. But Ride kept that aspect of her life hidden from most people.

Following Ride's death, there was much discussion in the **media** about her being gay. **Prejudice** against gay people was common throughout Ride's lifetime. O'Shaughnessy says Ride kept this part of her identity hidden so it wouldn't **complicate** her career. The US public may not have supported a gay astronaut in the 1980s.

After Ride's death, she continued to be honored for her life's work. **NASA** named a spot on the moon after her. The US Navy named a research ship the R/V *Sally Ride*.

In 2013, President Obama awarded Ride the Presidential Medal of Freedom. It is the nation's highest civilian honor.

After Ride's death, O'Shaughnessy published a children's book called *Sally Ride: A Photobiography of America's Pioneering Woman in Space.*

O'Shaughnessy accepted the award for Ride. This was the first time a same-sex partner did so. Many people saw this as a step forward for gay rights. Even after her death, Ride was blazing trails.

Lasting Impact

Ride was a hero to many people. Her historic spaceflight was a turning point at **NASA**. After that mission, more and more women were included in space travel. Today, NASA spaceflights include crews made up of both men and women. Many of these women say Ride was their role model.

Ride's influence spread far beyond NASA. She inspired countless women and girls who were interested in science. After her death, Ride also became an inspiration to the gay community as the first gay astronaut. A college friend thought Ride was ahead of her time in showing others she was their equal. He said Ride "**asserted** herself in a way that said, 'I'm here and I'm capable and I'm doing it.'"

Though Ride was famous and admired, she never looked for attention. Her focus was on the science and skill behind space exploration. Ride worked her entire life to further knowledge and interest in space. Her **legacy** lives on through the thousands of women who contribute to space exploration today.

STELLAR!
By July 2017, NASA had sent a total of 50 different women into space!

Ride will always be known for helping women succeed. She was even admitted into the National Women's Hall of Fame!

Timeline

Sally Kristen Ride is born on May 26 in Encino, California.
1951

Ride enrolls at Stanford University.
1970

Ride becomes a capsule communicator (CAPCOM) at NASA.
1981

1968
Sally graduates from Westlake High School for Girls.

1978
NASA chooses Ride for its astronaut program. Ride earns her PhD in physics later in the year.

Ride makes history on June 18 as the first US woman in space.

1983

Ride founds education company Sally Ride Science with four other women.

2001

Ride dies on July 23 from cancer.

2012

1984

Ride becomes the first US woman to travel into space for a second time.

1987

Ride leaves NASA and becomes director of the California Space Institute.

2003

Ride is admitted into the Astronaut Hall of Fame.

Glossary

assert—to speak or act in a way that draws people's attention.

aviation—the operation and navigation of aircraft.

bachelor's degree—a college degree that is usually earned after four years of study.

cancer—any of a group of often deadly diseases marked by harmful changes in the normal growth of cells. Cancer can spread and destroy healthy tissues and organs.

complicate—to make complex or difficult.

cosmos—the universe. enroll—to register, especially in order to attend a school.

enroll—to register, especially in order to attend a school.

feminist—a supporter of women's rights.

gender—the behaviors, characteristics, and qualities most often associated with either the male or female sex.

legacy—something important or meaningful handed down from previous generations or from the past.

master's degree—a college degree that is usually earned after one or two years of additional study following a bachelor's degree.

media—a form or system of communication, information, or entertainment. It includes television, radio, and newspapers.

NASA—National Aeronautics and Space Administration. NASA is a US government agency that manages the nation's space program and conducts flight research.

obituary—an article about the life of someone who has died.

PhD—doctor of philosophy. Usually, this is the highest degree a student can earn.

physics—a science that studies matter and energy and how they interact. A scientist who studies physics is a physicist.

prejudice—a negative opinion of a particular group based on factors such as race or religion.

satellite—a manufactured object that orbits Earth. It relays scientific information back to Earth.

semester—half of a school year.

sexist—unfair to someone because of her or his sex.

space walk—an activity in which an astronaut does work outside a spacecraft while it is in space.

thermal—related to heat.

ONLINE RESOURCES

Booklinks
NONFICTION
NETWORK
FREE! ONLINE NONFICTION RESOURCES

To learn more about Sally Ride, visit **abdobooklinks.com**. These links are routinely monitored and updated to provide the most current information available.

Index

A

astronaut training, 10
awards, 22, 24, 25

C

California, 6
California Space
  Institute, 20
Challenger, space shuttle,
  14, 16, 18
Clinton, Bill, 20, 22
Columbia, space shuttle,
  22

D

death, 24

E

education, 4, 6, 8, 10, 20,
  21, 24, 25

F

family, 6, 12, 14, 19, 20, 21,
  24, 25
female astronauts, 8, 10,
  11, 12, 16, 17, 26

K

Kennedy Space Center,
  14

M

media attention, 12, 14,
  15, 16, 24
milestones, 4, 14, 16, 22,
  25, 26
missions, 11, 12, 14, 16

N

National Aeronautics and
  Space Administration
  (NASA), 4, 8, 10, 11, 16,
  17, 18, 19, 20, 22, 24, 26

O

O'Shaughnessy, Tam, 6,
  14, 20, 21, 24, 25

P

Pennsylvania, 6

S

Sally Ride Science, 20
sexuality, 4, 24, 25, 26
sports, 4, 6, 8
Stanford University, 6,
  8, 10
Swarthmore College, 6

T

teaching, 20

W

Westlake High School for
  Girls, 6
writing, 4, 21, 22